CW01512937

Original title:
The Thread of Connection

Copyright © 2025 Creative Arts Management OÜ

Author: Matthew Whitaker

ISBN HARDBACK: 978-1-80586-029-7
ISBN PAPERBACK: 978-1-80586-501-8

Embraced by Harmony

In a world of socks that never mate,
I found a partner, isn't that great?
We laugh at chaos, dance in delight,
Two mismatched pairs that feel just right.

Life's laundry piles higher each day,
With spilled coffee and crumbs in the fray.
Yet our giggles weave through the mess,
Making the mundane feel a bit less.

Tapestry of Moments

A toaster burns bread with a sizzle and pop,
While I juggle pancakes that flop and drop.
We share a kitchen, it's always a riot,
Flour fights happen, there's no need to diet.

Our recipe's wild, a pinch of this,
A dash of laughter, we can't miss.
When dinner's a disaster, we just call for Thai,
And toast to the favorites that we can't fry.

Handcrafted Connections

With crayons and markers, we artfully mess,
Creating a mural that's pure genius, yes!
Mom says it's chaos, but we see the fun,
A wild masterpiece under the sun.

In glue and glitter, our stories unfold,
Each mishap and giggle, worth more than gold.
We'll frame our mischief, hang it on high,
Proving that laughter can always fly.

Weaving Our Stories

With knitting needles, we craft a new tale,
Of derailed stitches and laughter so pale.
My scarf turned to strands, it's wildly absurd,
Yet I wear my creation, flamboyantly blurred.

In the pub's warmth, with drinks all around,
We share our quirks, no need to be bound.
Our stories entwined in a comical spin,
Together we'll laugh, let the fun begin!

Fabric of Familiarity

In a world of socks and shifty shoes,
We trip on laughter, dodging blues.
Grab my hand, let's make a scene,
The fabric of us is stitched in green.

Unraveled tales of coffee spills,
With every sip, our chaos thrills.
You bring the jokes, I'll bring the snacks,
Together we'll steer through friendship's cracks.

Tapestry of Souls

Two peas in a pod, or maybe a pear,
Stuck in a blanket, we giggle and swear.
Your antics bizarre, mine a bit odd,
Crafting a bond that leaves us awed.

Colorful threads wrapped 'round our hearts,
A patchwork of laughter, where silliness starts.
We dance through the mundane, a silly parade,
In this tapestry, no moments fade.

Interlaced Journeys

With a map drawn in crayon, we wander and roam,
Finding new routes that feel like home.
Your car's on empty, my snack bag's bare,
But who needs gas when we've got flair?

Tangled in tales of misadventures,
Traveling roads with lack of censures.
The GPS may fail, but laughter is true,
In our interlaced journeys, it's always new.

Threads of Tomorrow

Tomorrow's fabric spins in delight,
As we weave our dreams by morning light.
Waking up late, coffee turns cold,
We laugh at the chaos, of friendship bold.

With mismatched socks and hair in a mess,
We step out together, no time to stress.
Each quirky moment, just right for replay,
Threads of tomorrow, we joyfully lay.

Interwoven Dreams

In a dream where socks do peek,
They mingle with my crazy week.
A snoring cat on top my head,
Convinces me to skip the bed.

The broom dances, sweeping dust,
A partner in this nightly thrust.
With giggles woven in the seams,
We laugh like kids, in crazy dreams.

Common Threads

We share a laugh over spilled juice,
And wonder if it's time to deduce.
The secrets of socks in hidden cracks,
And friendships built on midnight snacks.

My dog's insistence on daily runs,
Leaves me in stitches, oh the puns!
A belly ache from too much fun,
We chase the sun, we always run.

Bridges in the Ether

Like Wi-Fi signals that never break,
We ping thoughts in the silliest take.
Through memes and gifs we send a hug,
A virtual chat, all warm and snug.

Emails that land in spam's embrace,
We find connection in baffled grace.
A modern bond built on typed-out glee,
In digital realms, we're wild and free.

Frayed Ends of Belonging

We wear mismatched shoes to the parade,
Our silly quirks, in colors displayed.
A friendship formed on awkward swings,
Laughing at all the silly things.

With glue and tape, we fix our pride,
And dance on paths where love can guide.
Though frayed and worn, we stick like glue,
In every laugh, there's me and you.

Entwined Destinies

In a world where socks go missing,
Two mismatched pairs are reminiscing.
One lost its toe in a laundry fight,
While the other danced away one night.

Like tangled ears of earbuds, they laughed,
Each twist and turn, a silly draft.
"Oh look, I found a spoon instead!"
"Great, let's use it for our thread!"

Connections Unraveled

Two cats on a fence, plotting to pounce,
One just wanted to steal a bounce.
The other said, "Let's play a prank!"
But ended up in the neighbor's trunk.

A dog in a tutu, quite a sight,
Chasing its tail with all its might.
Losing the plot, it spun around fast,
Connecting with chaos, a comical blast!

Symphony of Strands

A moth to a flame, oh what a joke,
Dancing around till its wings went up in smoke.
It thought it'd join a disco tonight,
Now it's the star of a flameout flight.

Strings of spaghetti, twirl on a fork,
Some end up slipping and land with a squawk.
"Who knew this meal would start a fight?"
"In a saucy tango, we take our bite!"

Lattice of Life

Two hedgehogs met, prickly and shy,
Attempting a hug, oh my, oh my!
A snort, a roll, what a silly display,
"Let's connect minds, but stay far away!"

In a dance of noodles, the clumsy agreed,
Spaghetti linked with a hero's deed.
"Life's just a joke when you trip and fall,
But laughter's the glue that connects us all!"

Nexus of Hearts

From silly memes we share with grace,
To chords of laughter, we embrace.
In a world of pixels, we all glow,
With every click, our spirits grow.

Who knew friendship could be this strange?
With cats and GIFs, we rearrange.
In this digital web, we play our part,
Connecting souls with a wink, a heart.

Echoes Across Distance

Far apart, but never alone,
With voices chirping through the phone.
Jokes that span from here to there,
Across the miles, we share a chair.

We giggle at the quirks we know,
With every text, our humor flows.
In echoes of laughter, bonds are tight,
In this silly dance, we find delight.

Bound by Emotion

Through ups and downs, we ride the wave,
With inside jokes that we both crave.
In every tear, there's joy and grace,
With silly faces, we win the race.

In this mess of feelings we compose,
Like clumsy clowns in colorful clothes.
With chuckles binding us, we thrive,
In this lovely circus, we come alive.

Stitching Memories

With threads of laughter, we sew our tales,
We gather moments, not just sales.
In quirky patterns, our lives collide,
With every stitch, we take in stride.

From pizza nights to grabbing fries,
Hidden snacks under starry skies.
In this patchwork, love is our art,
With goofy smiles, we play our part.

Heartstrings and Vines

In a garden of giggles, we bloom and we sway,
With vines that tickle, leading us astray.
A dance with the daisies, we can't help but grin,
Each twist and each turn, where does chaos begin?

A squirrel in a top hat, he juggles his nuts,
While frogs croak out tunes that will give you the guts.
With laughter like raindrops, we splash in the mud,
As roots intertwine, we grow in the flood.

Old socks make for puppets, they chatter and cheer,
They plot little mischiefs, with no sign of fear.
With each silly prank, we can't help but shout,
In this quirky patch, there's no room for doubt.

So here's to the moments, the laughter entwined,
A jester's delight, joyfully maligned.
For life's a grand circus, where silly aligns,
And heartstrings are tangled like grapes on the vines.

Melodies of Affinity

In a world of tangled thoughts,
We dance like socks in dryers.
Each step is made of laughter,
While coffee brews in dryer fires.

Your jokes are like confetti,
Falling gently on my brain.
We harmonize like birds on wires,
Singing tunes to entertain.

When misunderstandings arise,
We take a break to laugh.
A pun here or a joke there,
Turns woes to comic gaffes.

So here's to us, a funny pair,
Like spoons and forks at tables.
United by our silly ways,
Only we can draw these fables.

Braided Hearts

Like spaghetti in a salad,
Tangled in a twisty knot.
Our hearts dance in mischief,
In a friendship that can't be bought.

You wear my favorite hoodie,
I sport your mismatched socks.
Together we're a circus,
Full of quirks and funny knocks.

Your tales are quite absurd,
Like squirrels with tiny hats.
In this charming world we've spun,
Laughter echoes like little bats.

We build our dreams like Lego blocks,
With laughter as our glue.
Each giggle that we share,
Makes our friendship feel new.

Shadows of Understanding

In shadows cast by high fives,
We trip on laughter's grace.
Your quirks are my bright lanterns,
Lighting up this silly space.

When life throws curveball pitches,
We laugh and try again.
Like two clowns in a circus,
No fear of cents or ten.

You spill tea and I spill beans,
In our secret joke parade.
Underneath the comet's glow,
We play the fun brigade.

From goofy glances to wild dances,
Our minds are quite a mix.
In this game of silly thoughts,
We craft our laughter tricks.

The Loom of Friendship

In the fabric of our laughter,
We weave our silly dreams.
Like kittens chasing shadows,
And racing down moonbeams.

Our jokes are woven tightly,
With threads of bright delight.
We tie our hearts with giggles,
In this raucous, joyful flight.

With every stitch of humor,
We patch the holes of gloom.
Crafting tales of pure nonsense,
That bloom like flowers in bloom.

So let's spin tales of friendship,
On this loom we love to share.
In the tapestry of our lives,
We're threads beyond compare.

Lonely Threads

In a box sat a needle, tired and worn,
She wished for a buddy, maybe a horn.
A spool of yarn chuckled, spun round and round,
"You can't sew a sock if you're homeward bound!"

But one day it happened, a button did roll,
Out of nowhere, it joined the whole scroll.
"What's your name?" asked the thread, with delight,
"I'm Button McBouncy, let's stitch up the night!"

Unbreakable Links

Two quirky beads danced on a string,
"Can you believe we spark joy?" they'd sing.
One was a gem, the other a rock,
"Together we shine, like a cuckoo clock!"

A paperclip joined, a real wild card,
"I'm not rubber, but I play hard!"
They twirled and they spun, a wacky parade,
Till a matchstick chimed in, "Let's throw a charade!"

Gypsy's Stitches

A mix of colors and patterns galore,
Her patchwork blankets were never a bore.
"Stitch me a unicorn, make it a beast!"
"How about a pizza?" she laughed, "that's the feast!"

With scissors in hand, and laughter to spare,
She snipped out some clouds, then gave them a hair.
"Look at us float, in the laughter we weave!"
"Who knew stitches could party and never deceive?"

The Weave of Us

Two threads were entangled, a dance quite absurd,
"Whose idea was this?" "Let's not say a word!"
They twisted and twirled like a couple in shock,
"Are we still friends?" they asked, cautious as rocks.

With giggles and snorts, they grew tight with delight,
"Tangled or not, we'll sew up the night!"
A knot that's most stubborn, yet full of pure cheer,
"Together forever, let's conquer this fear!"

Melting Boundaries

A cat in a hat, chasing a mouse,
Sipping tea in the neighbor's house.
Gloves that giggle, socks that dance,
Even spoons seem to prance.

Cakes that gossip, ice cream chats,
Jellybeans wearing party hats.
Cupcakes twisting in a cakewalk,
Cookies whispering silly talk.

Neighbors arguing over cake size,
While the garden grows jokes in disguise.
Lawn chairs link arms, giggling away,
As laughter blossoms, come what may.

Conversations in Stitches

Knitting needles click in a row,
Making sweaters that hilariously glow.
Purling dreams into cozy seams,
Blankets plotting seven schemes.

Grandma swears her yarn's alive,
Talking back, it helps her thrive.
Each knot a tale, each loop a jest,
Knitted secrets, never at rest.

Crochet hooks roll on the floor,
Stitching jokes we can't ignore.
A scarf that teases, a mitten that sings,
Crafting connections with silly strings.

Cosmic Intertwining

Stars do a jig in the cosmic sea,
Planets gossip, 'Did you see me?'
Meteor showers send texts from afar,
Spinning tales of where they are.

Galaxies giggle in spiraled fun,
Wormholes whisper, 'We're all one!'
Saturn juggling rings with flair,
While comets dance without a care.

Cosmic kites fly high in the sky,
Asteroids chuckle as they fly by.
In celestial bazaars, laughter rings,
As the universe strums on quirky strings.

Veins of Affinity

A vine that tickles the old oak tree,
Swaying lightly, just like me.
Branches gossiping in the breeze,
Filling the air with a dash of tease.

Roots intertwine beneath the ground,
Sharing secrets without a sound.
Plants prattle while daisies plot,
Sunflowers nod, giving it a thought.

Earthworms chuckle as they wriggle,
Each soil shift a quirky giggle.
Life connections in playful spree,
Nature's humor always sets us free.

Interlaced Dreams

In a world where socks go missing,
I dream of pairs that are not hissing.
Tangled tales of lost and found,
A wardrobe circus all around.

One sock tells jokes while the other sighs,
Taxing my patience with endless ties.
They leap and dance, a colorful sight,
Making laundry days a riotous night.

A shirt joins in, sporting a grin,
Laughing at battles where no one's a win.
Together they plot, oh what a mess,
Fashion faux pas, they simply confess.

So here's to threads that weave us near,
In laughter and love, with a touch of cheer.
In every tangle, there's a laugh to reap,
A fabric joke, buried oh so deep.

Handwritten Stories

In a world where pen meets page,
Wonders unfold, just like a stage.
Letters collide like curious friends,
Telling tales where humor never ends.

A cat wrote a novel, all about fish,
While a mouse scribbled dreams and a dastardly wish.
Together they bickered over dinner so grand,
A comedy of errors, oh what a plan!

Erasers became villains, plotting in vain,
To smudge every story, driving them insane.
But in laughter, they found rhythm and flow,
Handwritten chaos, a wild show.

So toss out the script, let ink run free,
Life's a funny tale for you and me.
Each handwritten story, a giggle or two,
A parchment of joy, just waiting for you.

Ties of Empathy

Two shoes lost in a dusty hall,
Tried to connect, just to have a ball.
One loved to dance, the other, to hop,
Together they bounced until one went plop!

Oh, the odd couple, a pair so bright,
One in a sneaker, the other in white.
They argued over steps, who led the way,
Yet when they tripped, they giggled, hooray!

A flip-flop chimed in, shouting, 'Let's sway!'
With laughter echoing, they danced away.
Stumbling and tumbling, all in good fun,
Bonded by blunders, under the sun.

So here's to shoes with eccentric flair,
A bond that's stitched through mistakes they share.
In every fallen arch, a lesson to glean,
Two mismatched soles creating a scene.

Stitched from Love

In a quilt of quirks, we find our peace,
Each square a laugh, like a joyful fleece.
Grandma's old patterns, a mix and a match,
Stitched with affection, a colorful batch.

A patch of bright sunshine, splashed with blue,
Next to it, a cat that's lost its shoe.
Every design tells a story so grand,
Of laughter and warmth, all intricately planned.

Some squares wrinkle, while others proudly shine,
But with every fold, they're still divine.
They wiggle and giggle, all snug and tight,
A cozy reminder, in day or night.

So here's to the stitches, the knots that we tie,
In moments of joy, we'll laugh and we'll cry.
Crafted from love, with care and some fun,
Each quilt a memory, for everyone.

Common Threads

In a world where socks go missing,
And sweater pets are ever-kissing,
We laugh at all the tangled fates,
As everyone debates on mates.

A zipper's gone, a button flies,
Lost in laughter, we realize,
That life's a quilt of patchy schemes,
Stitched together, backed by dreams.

From yarns of yarn that people spin,
To sharing crumbs from food within,
We weave our stories, day by day,
And poke fun at the fray's display.

So grab a thread, let's knit a joke,
A blanket made for laughter's smoke,
In fabric's folds, we'll dance and trot,
Finding humor in the knots.

Weaving Together Destiny

Two dandelions ride the breeze,
While ants declare, "We do as we please!"
Insects prance on paths unknown,
As fate rolls out its thread and bone.

Grandma's quilt becomes our map,
With patterns sewn on knees and lap,
Each patch a giggle, snicker, chime,
A riot of color, bold and prime.

Let's toss confetti, spin, and reel,
With glue-gun hearts that gladly feel,
In mishaps, gags, we find our way,
While threadbare jokes decide to stay.

Laugh with the stitches, snip the seams,
In this wacky world of mismatched dreams,
We weave our tales with silly flair,
Connected by moments light as air.

Ties That Bind

In cycling shorts, we ride along,
With shoelaces tied and guitars in song,
Tripping over tales, we stumble and fall,
Yet ties that bind hold the best of all.

Like playful cats in yarny fights,
Or mishaps born from poorly-tied kites,
Laughter echoes where we play,
In strands of crazy, come what may.

A friendship's sway, with mirth entwined,
In awkward hugs and snacks combined,
We laugh until our sides do ache,
Those ties of humor, can't break or shake.

So let's embrace the silly mess,
In every twist, we find our bliss,
Connected tightly, a vibrant bind,
Together we're hilariously aligned!

Unseen Fabrics

In silly hats, we dance through time,
In shirts with prints that barely rhyme,
An abstract art of joy and peace,
Unseen threads that never cease.

A weave of stories, all absurd,
Where laughter flies, and joy is stirred,
In mismatched patterns, bright and bold,
A fabric woven, stories told.

So each mishap becomes a stitch,
In life's grand quilt, a little glitch,
With every laugh, the fabric grows,
With silly fibers nobody knows.

Let's leap and twirl, in twinkling threads,
Where joy spills over, and laughter spreads,
In unseen fabrics, we find delight,
In quirky tales, we take flight.

Kintsugi of Relationships

In the mix of coffee spills,
Our laughter's sticky glue,
We fix each other's broken cups,
With shards of memories too.

A crack here, a dent there,
We wear them like fine art,
Every flaw a funny story,
Each break a punk rock heart.

Our bonds, like cracked ceramics,
Patching life with gold,
When we trip over each other,
We just laugh, not scold.

So raise a glass to mishaps,
To the chaos in our days,
For every cute disaster,
Is a line in our ballet.

Spirit Threads

We dance like tangled ribbons,
In a game of hide and seek,
Falling down is part of fun,
Each twist a giggle peak.

When you trip on my shoelaces,
And I steal your last fry,
Our spirit threads entwine deeply,
With every culinary cry.

We weave a tapestry of quirks,
From lost socks to wild hair,
Spinning tales of silly fights,
With a nudge and gentle stare.

So here's to our wild fibers,
In all their jumbled grace,
The clumsier the connection,
The funnier the embrace.

Gazes of Trust

Your funny look says it all,
When I forget the plan,
It's a mix of love and eye-rolls,
In our unpredictable span.

Those awkward moments shared,
Like sneezes at the wrong time,
Each glance, a wink of trust,
Makes life's chaos feel sublime.

When our thoughts seem tangled,
And words can go awry,
One raised eyebrow signals,
Our friendship's the reason why.

So keep your eyes wide open,
Let's laugh at every blunder,
For with each silly gaze,
We make life feel like thunder.

Ripple Effects

One laugh leads to another,
Like stones tossed in a pond,
Every chuckle is a ripple,
In the chaos, we respond.

A slip on a banana peel,
Turns into a dance so bright,
With every silly tumble,
We spark laughter like starlight.

Our giggles bounce like dolphins,
Across the waves of trust,
In each moment, little splashes,
Of joy that's so robust.

Join the beach of our nonsense,
Where smiles are freely tossed,
In the ocean of connection,
Not one wave is ever lost.

The Fabric of Us

In a world so stitched and sewn,
Pants mismatched, socks overgrown.
We thread our laughs through fabric tight,
Wearing joy with all our might.

Stitch by stitch, we seam together,
Laughing at mishaps, no need for leather.
With needle and thread, we dance and play,
Creating a masterpiece every day.

In a fabric shop, we found our groove,
Cutting patterns while we move.
Avoiding the pinprick, we're so clever,
In this quilt of life, we're super forever.

So here's to the ties that snugly weave,
With fabric scraps, we won't grieve.
Our laughter's stitched on every seam,
In the fabric of us, we reign supreme.

Woven Whispers

In a loom of giggles, secrets spun,
Whispers tangled, oh what fun!
A thread of humor, a stitch of grace,
We weave our tales in a happy place.

Each hair pulled out is a story told,
Knots of laughter as we grow old.
With every twist, a chuckle flows,
Woven whispers, where friendship glows.

Fabric of stories, truth or lie,
Stretched so far, we touch the sky.
In our quilted world, we take our stand,
With woven whispers, it's all so grand.

So let's conceal our silly fears,
With colorful yarn and happy cheers.
In threads entwined, our fate is set,
Laughing together, we'll never fret.

Tapestry of Souls

In a tapestry bright, where colors clash,
Knitting dreams in a hurried dash.
Each soul a thread, quirky and wild,
Binding us closely, forever a child.

With yarn that's frayed, we still keep score,
Dancing through errors, we always want more.
A patchwork of mishaps, both funny and grand,
In each little fiber, together we stand.

Stitching the moments, both silly and sweet,
In a fabric of laughter, we find our beat.
Sewing our past with a gleaming thread,
In this comedy quilt, we have nothing to dread.

So here's to the foolish and wild we pursue,
Tapestry of souls, vibrant and true.
With each little knot that we lovingly make,
Together we flourish, together awake.

Bonds Beyond Measure

In a realm of buttons and silly ties,
We dance with fabric that never lies.
A bond so stretchy, we laugh and play,
Measurement lost in our funny display.

From pants that rip to socks that slide,
Our humor fits like an oversized ride.
With every slip, our spirits rise,
In laughter's grip, we wear our prize.

Stitches entwined in a pattern so bright,
Crafting connections like stars at night.
Measuring hearts with a rubber band,
Bonds beyond measure, so perfectly planned.

So here's to the fabric of playful hearts,
In a lively quilt where the joy imparts.
Together we gather, creating our treasure,
In bonds that exceed all standard measure.

Embers of Connection

Around the campfire, we laugh and joke,
The marshmallows burn, as we share our poke.
With stories of past, and future dreams bright,
We roast our worries, till late into night.

Each silly dance, a spark of delight,
With laughter so loud, we take to the flight.
Guitars strum tunes, a cacophony sung,
In this funny chaos, our hearts feel so young.

No need for a map, to find where we stand,
In pranks and in banter, we form a new band.
Our jests weave a fabric, peculiar yet bold,
In the warmth of the fire, our stories unfold.

So let's raise a glass, to the quirks we adore,
In this mixed-up design, we always want more.
Like embers that flicker, our spirits align,
Together in laughter, perfectly fine.

Silhouette of Togetherness

Under the streetlamps, we act like fools,
With shadows that dance, ignoring the rules.
A conga line forms, with a wobble and sway,
In the dark of the night, we all find a way.

To trip over shoes, and stumble on air,
In the hubbub of friendship, there's humor to share.
Each slip and each fall, becomes part of our lore,
With giggles that echo, we always want more.

We reenact scenes, from movies so grand,
Aliens, monsters, the whole silly band.
With every strange pose, we capture the night,
In the silliness lived, we find pure delight.

So let's not forget, the joy that we feed,
In our odd silhouettes, we plant a good seed.
Together we bloom, like flowers in spring,
Creating a garden, that laughter can bring.

Genesis of Bonds

In the chaos of life, we stumble and trip,
But all of our quirks, just add to the zip.
With every 'oops' and each funny glance,
We build up our bonds, as we jiggle and dance.

From awkward small talk, to silly charades,
We craft this bond, in humorous shades.
With snorts and with giggles, and belly laughs galore,
Each moment together, just opens the door.

Like magnets we cling, with a pull that's quite strong,
In this playful ballet, we never feel wrong.
We share our mishaps, in comical ways,
Creating a tapestry, of fun-filled days.

So here's to the starts, we make each bright morn,
In this beautiful mess, a new friendship is born.
With smiles like confetti, we fill every space,
In this genesis of bonds, we all find our place.

Mosaic of Memories

Each laugh a tile, in our quirky design,
Fitting together, like cheese and good wine.
We puzzle through life, with a piece here and there,
In this mosaic of memories, we always share.

From faces all funny, to stories afoot,
In the garden of goofs, we flourish and root.
With every odd venture, we matter and shine,
Painting our lives, with colors divine.

We sketch out the plans, for adventures ahead,
Like kids chasing dreams, with nothing to dread.
The laughter like glue, it sticks us so tight,
In this canvas of chaos, we feel so right.

So here's to the mishaps, the laughter, the cheer,
In this mosaic of memories, we hold all dear.
Every quirky shade, every wacky hue,
Together we shine, in all that we do.

Stitches of Time

In a world where socks go missing,
I search for pairs without dismissing.
Life's a quilt of little laughs,
With silly patterns and quirky gaffes.

My grandma knits while watching TV,
Creating chaos with glee, you see.
Each stitch a story, each purl a cheer,
We dance through yarn, my friends, my dear.

Little yarn balls roll on the floor,
Chasing them, I laugh and roar.
She yells, 'Stop, or it'll knot!'
But I trip and fall, with quite a plot!

Yet through the fabric of our shared days,
We weave our lives in merry plays.
Threading joy in every room,
Like socks, we create our own bloom.

Intertwined Journeys

Two llamas met on the grand road,
One had a map, the other, a load.
"Are we lost?" the first one brayed,
"Not if we follow the ice cream parade!"

We stumbled through fields of wild flowers,
Turning our trip into laughter hours.
With every misstep, every surprise,
We painted the world with giggly eyes.

A raccoon joined in for a snack,
Claiming the treasure from my backpack.
"Hey, buddy, lunch is for two!"
But he just grinned, popping in a shoe.

Through paths that twisted like silly straws,
We embraced the chaos with joyful paws.
Though maps may tear and plans may sway,
We dance through life, come what may.

Echoes of Affection

In a café, we argue on scones,
Who knew dough could lead to groans?
"Oh, they're too dry!" the other protests,
"Perhaps your taste is what's a jest!"

With crumbs and giggles all over the place,
We enjoy the crumbs that match our grace.
Every bite sparks a chuckle or two,
Love layered thick like our pastry crew.

We share secrets over teacups small,
Like sugar cubes that rise and fall.
With every sip, our hearts collide,
In silly tales, we choose to confide.

Underneath the laughter, a bond so deep,
It's all the memories we love to keep.
A little chaos, a sprinkle of fun,
With each echo, our hearts are one.

Frayed Edges of Belonging

My shirt's unraveling, a loose thread!
It leads to adventures instead.
"Fix it!" my mother gives me a stare,
But I chuckle as I twirl in mid-air.

At the park, I meet a cat named Pie,
"Are you a snack?" I ask with a sigh.
He purrs, "Let's find those threads we've lost,
Life's too fun to think of the cost."

Together we chase ribbons in the breeze,
As we laugh and tumble with such ease.
Our friendship's a fabric, a patchwork delight,
Sewn in giggles that sparkle so bright.

With frayed edges, we're perfectly sewn,
In this quirky world, we've fully grown.
Crazy moments will keep us strong,
In the hall of fun, it's where we belong.

Dances of Togetherness

In a room full of cats, we twirl and spin,
With purrs as our rhythm, we begin again.
The allergies come, but who gives a hoot?
We dance 'round the furniture, in socks and a boot.

Laughter erupts, what a silly sight,
We kick up the dust and we're feeling just right.
The neighbors complain, but we just won't hear,
For everyone knows, it's the laughter we cheer.

Bouncing like bunnies, we trip and we tum,
A conga line forms, and we've got a drum.
The cookies we baked send us running fast,
Who needs a dance floor? We're having a blast!

So join us next time, catch some catnip high,
We'll make a big mess and then eat pie!
With giggles and wiggles, we'll shake up the place,
In our dance of together, we're winning the race.

Blueprint of Belonging

We gathered 'round the table, maps all spread wide,
The blueprint of fun, with friends as our guide.
A game of Jenga, oh what a mess,
One block too high? What a great stress!

We plot our next move, with snacks on the side,
With laughter erupting; it's an adventurous ride.
Who made the decision? It's all out of whack,
But laughter we share... let's just cover the snacks!

The cat jumps right in, knocking it flat,
The pieces go flying; imagine that!
We giggle and argue, then strategize more,
With a friendship this strong, who could ask for more?

So grab your blueprints, let's build something bright,
With humor and chaos, we'll turn wrongs to right.
In this journey of ours, up and then down,
We're sharing this life; we're the fun-loving crowd.

Notes in the Weave

With threads of our tales, we stitch and we sew,
Each laugh a sharp note; our friendships do grow.
A fumble with yarn, it knottingly slips,
A yarn-bombed couch? Enjoy those funny quips!

We create quite the mess, with colors so bold,
Patterns of laughter in stories retold.
Who knew that the dog would run off with a skein?
Together, we cherish the joy and the pain.

Like notes in a song, we play our sweet part,
In rhythm we join, with warmth in our heart.
From stitches to laughter, each moment, a seam,
In this tapestry woven, we dance in a dream.

So give it a tug, see how it holds tight,
In this oopsie adventure, we take a delight.
With notes of our stories, let the music play,
In the weave of our lives, we'll dance every day.

Fabric of Resilience

In the fabric of life, we poke and we prod,
With stitches of humor, together we trod.
The quilt might be lumpy, with patches so bright,
But bound by laughter, it feels just right.

We patch up our worries, with fabric and thread,
Each rip a reminder, of all we have said.
The cat steals our needles, oh what a scene,
In this crazy chaos, we're living the dream.

When life throws a curve, we don't fall apart,
With seams of connection, we gather our heart.
Hey, who left the glue stick? It's stuck to my shoe!
We laugh at the troubles, together we brew.

So here's to the fabric, we stitch every day,
With laughter as color, in our quirky display.
We seam it all together, our quilt will survive,
With each little moment, we feel so alive!

Unity in Diversity

In a world so wide and bright,
People gather, what a sight!
A blend of laughs, a pinch of cheer,
Together we dance, let's grab a beer!

From tacos to sushi, the plate's a mess,
Each bite a joy, no need to stress.
We argue and bicker, then laugh it out,
Together we're stronger, that's what it's about!

In mismatched socks, we kick our feet,
Celebrate quirks, oh what a treat!
With stories wild and anecdotes grand,
Our jumbled lives do just expand!

So raise your voice with a chuckle or two,
In this riot of colors, there's room for you.
Together we shine, each one unique,
In this frolicsome life, let's take a peek!

Echoes Through Time

Once upon a time, a cat wore a hat,
It whispered secrets to a friendly bat.
Together they schemed, for what, we don't know,
Maybe a dance-off or a jellybean row!

Each story flows, from lips to ears,
With laughter and joy, and a few silly tears.
The past is a joke, a playful prank,
Echoes of laughter in an ancient tank!

A snail shares a tale, a turtle's delight,
Of how they had raced, a most friendly fight.
Each twist of fate, a giggle, a grin,
Together we learn where the fun can begin!

Time rolls on, but voices stay bright,
In laughter woven, day turns to night.
We shape our stories under the sky,
Together we soar, like birds flying high!

Portraits of Togetherness

With crayons we scribble, our laughter is loud,
Each stroke a memory, we stand out proud.
A portrait of pals, in mismatched attire,
A picture of joy, we never tire!

In a world of chaos, we find our bliss,
With goofy grins and a big ol' kiss.
From pie fights to pranks, we paint it bright,
Together we create our own delight!

Hand in hand, we stumble and trip,
Each blooper a treasure, oh what a flip!
We gather these moments, soak in the fun,
Under the glow of a cartoonish sun!

A canvas of life, so wild and free,
In this masterpiece, just you and me.
When colors collide, a vibrant blend,
In laughter and chaos, our joys ascend!

Harmony in Fragmentation

In snippets of laughter, we find our groove,
A mixed-up tune that makes us move.
With jumbled lyrics, oh what a sight,
We sing out loud, our fears take flight!

Among broken pieces, there's unity here,
Each shard a story, we hold dear.
With clumsy steps on this quirky path,
We stumble together, then burst into laugh!

In a puzzle of quirks, we fit just right,
Each part a missing piece, that ignites the night.
Together we jam, offbeat yet fine,
With laughter our anthem, we brightly shine!

So here's to the fragments, wild and free,
In the chaos and joy, there's magic, you see.
Finding harmony in laughter's embrace,
We're all just a stitch in this comical race!

Interwoven Paths

We walked the same old road, you see,
With shoes that squeaked like a symphony.
You tripped on a crack and nearly fell,
But laughed it off, time to cast a spell.

Our paths crisscross in quirky ways,
Like spaghetti in a giant maze.
You tried to be cool, but then you slipped,
Bumping into dogs, your plans all quipped.

A turtle raced by, oh what a sight,
We cheered it on, giving it might.
Our journey's wacky, wild, and bright,
Two friends in chaos, what pure delight!

So here's to the times that bind us tight,
Through laughter and fails, from day to night.
With every mishap, we shout with glee,
What a fun ride, just you and me!

Kinship in Kindness

You borrowed my shirt, I borrowed your comb,
Stitching life together, it feels like home.
We swap funny stories, from work and play,
Each one more absurd, brightening our day.

You spilled your drink, I made a splash,
We laughed so hard, neighbors thought it rash.
And every mishap brings us closer near,
With laughter as glue, there's nothing to fear.

Recycling old jokes like it's fine cheese,
We share fits of giggles, with perfect ease.
Your quirky dance moves could make a king stare,
And I join right in, with barely a care.

Through all of life's quirks that align like stars,
Our friendship's a wild, open car with no bars.
In kindness we thrive, with a wink and grin,
This bond's the true treasure, let the fun begin!

Textures of Life

Life's a patchwork quilt, stitched with flair,
A bit of this, and a sprinkle of hair.
Each fabric a tale, we giggle and pry,
Stumbling our way through the how and why.

A corduroy laugh and velvet mistake,
We dance through the chaos, for friendship's sake.
With polka dots dreams and stripes so bold,
Each moment together is pure pot of gold.

You wore mismatched socks to the fanciest ball,
And I brought a cat who just wanted to crawl.
In mismatched attire, we twirled and we spun,
To the laughter of all, we were just having fun.

So here's to the textures that weave our days,
With giggles and mishaps in quirky ways.
Together we're strong, in this fabric of fate,
A patchwork of joy that we celebrate!

Tie the Knot

We tied our shoes, what a silly sight,
One lace too long, the other too tight.
You ran in circles, I just fell flat,
But laughter erupted, how about that?

A double knot for the twists and bends,
Life's knotty confusion just never ends.
You tangled your words, tripping on fun,
Our friendship's a game that's just begun.

Your tie was a noose, my belt a bit loose,
We played dress-up in the wildest truce.
With each little blunder, we'd high-five tight,
Tangled together, all feels just right.

So here's to the knots that bind and conspire,
Through laughter and mishaps, we never tire.
Let's tie them tighter, on this crazy ride,
Two fools on a journey, with joy as our guide!

Weaving Light

In a room full of laughter, we spin our tales,
Each story a stitch, through the giggles it trails.
Bright yarns of chaos, tangled and fun,
We weave a bright fabric, all under the sun.

With needles of humor, we craft our delight,
Needles that poke from the left and the right.
Colors that clash, yet somehow unite,
In this wacky creation, everything's bright.

Together we whirl, like a dance in the breeze,
We toss and we tangle, with such silly ease.
The fabric of joy swings like a kite,
Flapping and fluttering, oh what a sight!

So let's raise a glass to our comradeship here,
A patchwork of laughter, let's make it clear.
In this wobbly world where we're bound through the
night,
Each chuckle a stitch, in our fabric so light.

Knots of Kindred Spirits

Oh look at us here, tangled in cheer,
Knots of connection, we hold oh so dear.
With goofy little faces and mismatched socks,
We tie ourselves tightly, like crafty old fox.

Like shoelaces knotted, we trip as we go,
But laughter's our glue, and all hearts aglow.
With the twist of a pun, we bind us with ease,
Creating a concoction that's sure to appease.

Our tangle of stories, a jumble delight,
Each loop that we make, spins the world just right.
From the creek to the fridge, we wander in rhyme,
A knotty escapade, we'll make it in time.

So here's to the knots, may they never come loose,
In this yarn of connection, we joyfully truce.
With each quirky twist, our spirits ignite,
Like a dance on the strands, we laugh through the night.

Invisible Bonds

Invisible threads, where mischief stirs,
We dance like marionettes, with silly purrs.
An eyebrow raised here, a wink over there,
It's all in the way, we sway without care.

Tugging and pulling, without any strings,
We're boisterous sprites, with our own little wings.
In a world of blunders, we cheerfully dwell,
With our bonds so invisible, we weave our own spell.

From breakfast shenanigans, to late-night plots,
Our laughter ignites, and connects all the dots.
Through the whispers of joy, and the giggles we breed,
These invisible ties are a magical creed.

So let's toast to the ties, that no one can see,
They hold us so snug, like a warm cup of tea.
A spark of connection, shared laughter our crown,
With bonds oh so silly, we never back down.

Weft of Understanding

In the loom of our lives, we weave and we play,
Each fiber a jest, in a funny ballet.
With threads of insight, we joke and we jive,
Matching our yarn, to keep the fun alive.

Playing with puns like a cat with a ball,
Bravado and shenanigans, we welcome them all.
With each twist and turn, we giggle and ponder,
The fabric of friendship bounds us like thunder.

Our tapestry drapes, with colors so bright,
Stitches of laughter, they twinkle at night.
Through the weft of our hearts, we thread gently through,
In this crazy quilt world, just bringing light to the blue.

So gather your yarn and find a snazzy seat,
Join our grand crafting with laughter replete.
In the loom we create, with humor as glue,
The weft of understanding, ties me to you.

Woven Whispers

In a world full of yarn, the cats conspire,
Plotting mischief with mischievous fire.
They twirl around legs, causing a mess,
Maybe it's all part of their playful jest.

With each little tangle, a laugh might erupt,
As they chase their own shadows, all bound up.
A knot here and there, oh what a show,
Weaving laughter wherever they go.

Invisible threads pull as the humor flows,
A tickling tale that nobody knows.
So join in their antics, let out a cheer,
For whispers of joy are always near.

So if you see a cat, take heed of the fun,
In every little thread, they've already won.
A bond made of laughter, spun light as a dream,
In this woven world, we're all part of the scheme.

Ties That Bind

There once was a sock with a mind of its own,
It vanished like magic, oh where had it flown?
From the laundry basket, it took a grand leap,
Leaving its partner in a pile, so deep.

This solo sock laughed at its sibling's despair,
'While you're stuck in the wash, I'm off to a fair!'
With a hop and a skip, it danced out the door,
To mingle with shoes and socks who danced on the floor.

Meanwhile, the left sock looked lonely and sad,
Wondering why fate made it feel so bad.
Then a parade of mismatched joined in with glee,
Creating a party for the lonely to see.

They wiggled and jiggled, these socks of all kinds,
Loosening their seams and abandoning binds.
In the end, they all found a joy that combined,
A collection of stories, all whimsically lined.

Strands of Silence

Two turtles sat quietly, sporting a grin,
They sent each other thoughts, from within.
As silence enveloped, they shared a good chuckle,
Each wriggling their toes in a cheerful huckle.

One turtle said, 'I think I might race!'
The other just snorted, 'At what kind of pace?'
With shells tied together, they stumbled along,
Each misstep a giggle, they couldn't go wrong.

A strand of connection in every clumsy turn,
With laughter like bubbles, they both took their burn.
In a world of slow-moving, they felt quite spry,
Though bonds weren't visible, oh my, oh my!

For in silent adventures, they shared in delight,
Bonded by humor that felt just so light.
Together they wandered, a most silly team,
Finding joy in the stillness, as laughter would gleam.

Unseen Links

A pair of old shoes, oh how they have danced,
With each step unwinding, they've often pranced.
A tip-toe, a shuffle, a shuffle, a sway,
Their laces entwined in a humorous way.

They chuckled at puddles and dodged every leaf,
Each adventure together was filled with belief.
Though one shoe was scuffed and the other was neat,
They explored all the streets and felt quite the feat.

'Hey buddy,' said the left shoe, with a wink,
'Without me, you'd surely miss the link!'
The right shoe chuckled, 'This is quite a pair,
With goofy companions, we've nothing to wear!'

So they tread on together, a duo of fun,
Forever connected, they surely have run.
For in every step, there's a story to spin,
Of unseen links and the joy found within.

Woven in Whimsy

In tangled yarns we play our games,
Frolicking with mismatched aims.
A sock that's lost, a hat that's bold,
Our quirky crafts they never get old.

With laughter's thread, we stitch and cheer,
Creating chaos, spreading good cheer.
An accidental scarf, an extra leg,
Our silly weavings make us beg.

From frayed edges, new joy will spring,
We laugh at all the quirks we bring.
Unraveled strands, yet all is well,
In our silly world, we weave and dwell.

So let us gather, let's make a mess,
For nothing's quite like our craftiness!
When laughter's the glue in our woven tale,
Life's a funny stitch, we never fail.

Hand in Hand

With gluey fingers, we craft and stick,
Who knew crafting could be so slick?
We pieced together odds and ends,
In our workshop, laughter transcends.

You drop a bead, I spill some glue,
We giggle at the mess we both pursue.
The pom-pom rolls, oh what a chase,
Hand in hand, we quicken our pace.

We mix the colors, a vibrant sight,
Looks like a rainbow got into a fight!
Yet from this jumbled, jolly array,
Our friendship sparkles, come what may.

So here's to us, the crafty pair,
With each mishap, we declare:
Hand in hand, we'll stitch and play,
Creating memories, come what may.

Heart to Heart

Two hearts that beat in crafty delight,
With glitter and glue, we take to flight.
Your heart's a button, mine's a lace,
Together, we're a joyful embrace.

We needle and thread, with giggles galore,
A painting made from hearts we adore.
When patterns clash, we just shake our head,
Real art is chaos, as genius has said!

With every stitch, our bond grows tight,
Laughter echoing through the night.
A heart-shaped mess, oh what a treat,
With you my friend, it's never a feat.

So here's to us, heart to heart,
In this fabric of whimsy, we're never apart.
Our thread may tangle, our paths may twist,
But in this grand weave, you're the joy I can't miss.

Approach to Kindred Spirits

When kindred spirits meet to weave,
It's laughter that we retrieve.
With scissors sharp and yarn askew,
Our creation is a colorful brew.

In wild patterns, we intertwine,
Crafting stories, so divine.
You craft a hat that fits a cat,
I top it off with a feathered bat!

Unruly threads make the best design,
In whimsical art, our souls align.
For every stitch and giggly fall,
Together we create, we enthrall!

Through every snip and playful tangle,
Our hearts are woven tight, they dangle.
So let's create, you and I,
With laughter echoing, let spirits fly.

Patterns in the Weave

In our funny twist of fate,
The patterns we create are first-rate!
Socks that don't match, that's our flair,
Each quirk and hiccup fills the air.

Like waffle cones stuffed with beans,
Our craftiness reigns in silly scenes.
You painted stripes on a polka dot,
A masterpiece that can't be caught!

We spin our tales, no need for sleep,
Stitches jump, in laughter we leap!
With every row, a new surprise,
Our patchwork hearts are quite the prize.

So grab your glue and let's create,
In this masterpiece, let's celebrate!
For in our funny, jumbled weave,
The bonds we forge, we won't believe!

Threads of Dreams

In a world where socks go stray,
Wishing they could dance away.
But laundry's a chaotic game,
Where missing pieces bear the blame.

We weave our hopes with yarn so bright,
Yet tangle pathways in the night.
Each twist and knot brings laughter near,
As wild creations reappear.

A dream once grand now just a shoe,
But laugh, we must; what else to do?
The silliness of fashion's grind,
Is threaded through our very mind.

Spiral of Emotions

Round and round emotions spin,
Like spaghetti on a fork, so thin.
You taste joy, then a dash of dread,
Swirl it all and toss your head.

Pasta dreams in ricotta rain,
Where happiness feels like a strain.
But guilt's just sauce that drips and falls,
As laughter echoes through the halls.

A twist of fate, a curve of cheese,
Life's a pizza, if you please.
With toppings wild and flavors bold,
Just serve it warm, and watch it unfold.

Love's Intricate Map

Maps are drawn with heart-shaped ink,
Yet lost directions make us think.
We wander through the fields of hope,
In search of where we long to grope.

Each 'X' marks places we've ignored,
Yet treasure lies where hearts are stored.
With arrows pointing every way,
We giggle as we save the day.

Compasses spin in silly whirls,
While we chase after flag-waving girls.
In love's terrain, we bravely roam,
Like kids who still call playgrounds home.

Doubles of Thought

Thoughts that bounce like rubber balls,
Hitting walls and answering calls.
One moment serious, then a jest,
These tangents put our minds to rest.

Double takes and tangled dreams,
We find ourselves in goofy schemes.
Logic laughs and logic cries,
As we ponder what underlies.

One thought leads to another's game,
Each new twist ignites a flame.
With every giggle, every sigh,
Our mind's a circus, oh my, oh my!

Fabric of Unity

In a world stitched with laughter,
Each patch tells a joke and a bluster.
With threads of silliness intertwined,
We share our quirks, all well-refined.

A button popped, oh what a sight!
The seams unravel, causing delight.
Through tangled yarns, we find a way,
To weave our joys, come what may.

A sock once lost, now a dance!
It twirls around, given a chance.
In cozy knit, our hearts convene,
Stitching memories that gleam and sheen.

Together we laugh, we poke, we prod,
In this fabric of fray, we find our nod.
So here's to the quilt of our silly jest,
Where unity sparks and we're at our best!

The Colors of Us

In shades of mischief, we blend our hues,
A palette of quirks, we cannot refuse.
With splashes of laughter, painted bright,
Our colors collide in the broad daylight.

A fuchsia joke, a neon pun,
With every giggle, we double the fun.
In this mismatched rainbow, we shine so bold,
Our goofy hearts, a sight to behold!

Cerulean dreams and tangerine schemes,
We craft our stories in vibrant themes.
With whimsical brushstrokes, we unite,
In the canvas of life, oh what a sight!

Together we paint, using whimsy and cheer,
Each stroke a memory, vibrant and clear.
So here's to the colors that spark such delight,
In this art of connection, we take flight!

Twists of Togetherness

In the spiral of giggles, we twist and turn,
With humor as fuel, together we learn.
A knot here and there, we playfully twine,
In this dance of antics, we all feel fine.

With a pirouette and a witty remark,
We spin our tales, igniting a spark.
In this funky formation, we laugh and giggle,
Our bond gets stronger with every wiggle.

A loop-de-loop kind of cooperation,
Wrapping around in our shared elation.
As we twist, we bend, and sometimes we fall,
But together, oh together, we always stand tall!

In the dance of our lives, we find a way,
To twine through the mess, come what may.
So let's keep spinning in this joyous spree,
Where each twist unites you and me!

Threads of Fate

With a wink and a nudge, destiny knits,
In this tapestry of life, we're all tiny bits.
A snarl here, a twist there, oh what a fuss,
But laughter unravels the tension for us.

We dangle on strings like puppets of cheer,
Making merry mischief, year after year.
In a hilarious dance, we jive and we sway,
Threads of our fates, all in disarray.

A tangle of socks or a mismatched shoe,
Every stumble reminds us of what's true.
That fate's just a game and we're players at heart,
With chuckles and giggles, we each play our part.

So let's sway with the silks and dance with delight,
In this fabric of fate, our futures are bright.
Together we laugh at the quirks we create,
For in every twist, we embrace our fate!

Unity in Diversity

In a land of socks and shoes,
Llama hats and quirky clues.
Each one's odd, just take a look,
Together, we're a wacky book.

Cats and dogs on leashes meet,
Dancing goofy to the beat.
Funny faces, silly grins,
Unity where laughter wins.

Colors clash, but we all shine,
Mixing up like cheese and wine.
A melting pot of playful quirks,
Where each one of us just smirks.

Like a pizza, full of zest,
Toppings weird, but still the best.
Together we'll have lots of fun,
In this big laugh—a everyone!

Strands of Tomorrow

With spaghetti hairdos and jellybeans,
We fashion dreams from silly scenes.
Tomorrow calls, let's paint it right,
With laughter and a twinkling light.

Sock puppets walk a funny line,
Tell tall tales of cheese and brine.
Every twist, a story told,
Laced with laughter, bright and bold.

Building bridges made of pie,
Plenty of smiles as we fly by.
With giggles as the ties we weave,
A tapestry that won't deceive.

When we share our funny quirks,
The future sparkles, laughter lurks.
In every joke, a bond we find,
Together, we expand the mind!

Bonds of Understanding

With rubber chickens and silly hats,
We share our thoughts, like acrobats.
Understanding grows with every jest,
In this circus, we're truly blessed.

A dance-off with our socks askew,
We spin and twist, like rubber glue.
In crazy moves, we find a way,
To see the world in shades of play.

Pickle juice and ice cream dreams,
Through laughter, every friendship beams.
A bond that's strong, yet light as air,
Comedic flair, it's truly rare!

When life gets tough and checks are due,
A punchline shared can pull us through.
So raise a grin, let laughter sing,
In this funny life, we're kings!

Hand in Hand

With fingers crossed, we skip along,
Singing silly, goofy songs.
Hand in hand, through thick and thin,
We'll laugh and twirl, let the fun begin!

Like pancakes flipping in the air,
Spreading joy without a care.
We twirl like napkins in the breeze,
Together, life's a big tease!

With silly dances, we take a stand,
Harmony in a wobbly band.
Each silly step, a rhythmic chance,
To share a laugh, and jiggle and prance.

So take my hand, let's dance away,
In this crazy, funny ballet.
Hand in hand, we can explore,
A world of fun, forevermore!

Patterns of Togetherness

We dance in circles, what a sight,
Like socks in a dryer, out of spite.
Each pirouette a tangled tale,
In this wobbly world, we'll never fail.

We swap our stories, over coffee spilled,
With laughter that echoes, hearts are thrilled.
Like quirky quilts from mismatched seams,
We patch our lives with joyful dreams.

When plans go awry, we just laugh it off,
Our friendship's a sitcom, no need for scoff.
In silly moments, we find our glue,
Like peanut butter, spread thick and true.

We paint our days with colors bright,
A rainbow of mishaps, pure delight.
In this dance of chaos, we find our way,
Together we giggle, come what may.

Underneath the Surface

Beneath the waves, we paddle and splash,
Like ducks on a pond, we dash and crash.
With ducks in a row and fish out of line,
We wrangle our worries, down we twine.

Caught in the net of our own wild tales,
Like sardines in a can, we giggle and flail.
Underneath the surface, we swim and weave,
In shoals of mishaps, we never leave.

We find hidden treasures in laughter's embrace,
Like crabs trying salsa, we wiggle with grace.
Bubbles of joy rise to the top,
In our quirky dance, we'll never stop.

Through ripples and waves, we splash in cheer,
In this sea of friendship, we have no fear.
With fins and a giggle, we ride the tide,
In the ocean of laughter, we glide side by side.

Bridge of Hearts

We built a bridge with popsicle sticks,
A crazy construction that often tricks.
With glue that's sticky and laughter loud,
We hold each other up, oh so proud.

Our hearts are cables, strung high above,
Wobbling like jelly, filled with love.
Each little heartbeat a funny tune,
A symphony played by the light of the moon.

We skip across, careful not to fall,
Like tightrope walkers, we giggle and brawl.
In this balancing act, we tread with glee,
One misstep, and it's a splash in the sea!

Hand in hand, we sway like the breeze,
A bridge of connection that's sure to please.
When the winds get strong, we hold on tight,
Laughing our way through the wobbly night.

The Fabric of Echoes

In the loom of laughter, we weave our dreams,
With threads of humor, bursting at the seams.
Each giggle a stitch, each chuckle a patch,
Creating a fabric no one can snatch.

Echoes of friendship bounce off the walls,
Like clumsy dance moves at goofy balls.
We twirl and we tumble, stitching our fate,
In this joyful quilt, we celebrate.

The fabric unravels, then mends with grace,
Like socks in the dryer at a frantic pace.
We patch up each hole with laughter and care,
In this wacky world, there's always a pair.

So here's to the fabric we stitch with bliss,
A tapestry woven with giggles and kiss.
In the echoes of joy, we find our song,
Together, forever, where we all belong.

Ethereal Weavings

In a web of giggles, we all do spin,
Our laughter's the glue, thick as skin.
We bounce like rubber, no worries in sight,
Chasing our shadows, oh what a delight!

With threads made of puns, we craft silly lace,
Frogs bounce in tuxedos, what a sight to face!
We tangle in jokes, it's a game we play,
Time flies on wings of a merry ballet!

A jester in each heart, joy is the plan,
We dance like wild flowers in a breezy fan.
Friends are the stitches, quirky and bright,
Knitting our dreams in the soft starlight!

So let's raise a glass, to the mishaps we weave,
In this fabric of fun, oh, can you believe?
We're tangled in smiles, together we stand,
Laughing and twirling in this goofball land!

Unity in Motion

In a land where socks dance, and spoons do tap,
Cats wear sunglasses, oh, what a mishap!
We roll through the chaos, like marbles in bowls,
With friends as our anchors, we bubble like shoals!

Our quirks are the beats that we all have to share,
Like squirrels in a circus, juggling with flair.
With each silly slip, our laughter does soar,
Bonding with giggles, who could ask for more?

In a race of oddities, we all take a spin,
Capped by our laughter, let the fun begin!
We stroll through the madness, a parade of glee,
Wobbling through life, as wild as can be!

So grab your odd pair, let's dance through the day,
With snacks in our pockets, come what may!
Each step's a story, won't you take a chance?
In this comedy chaos, together we prance!

Weft and Warp of Lives

In quirky patterns, we weave and we spin,
With mismatched buttons, life's oddball win.
We patch up our flaws with ribbons and cheer,
Strutting like peacocks, we laugh loud and clear!

Our tales are like fabrics, frayed at the seams,
Embroidered with silly, absurd little dreams.
We quilt every moment, with hiccups and snorts,
Turn blunders to treasures, our joyful retorts!

With each clumsy step, a new stitch is formed,
From chaos to craft, we gladly transformed.
We dance through the weft, and twirl through the warp,
Crafting our lives like an off-key harp!

So raise up your glasses, to this wacky affair,
With yarns of friendship, we've plenty to share!
We'll knit with a smile, and purl all the fun,
In this fabric of nonsense, we've only begun!

Celestial Connections

In a galaxy of giggles, we roam like the stars,
With comets of laughter and sandwiches far!
Jumping on sunbeams, as we float through the night,
In this cosmic dance, everything feels right!

We twirl with the planets, and juggle the moons,
Crafting tales of cheer that float to the tunes.
We're friends in this orbit, through thick and through thin,

Shooting for laughter - let the fun time begin!

So let's pass the popcorn, the universe wide,
With sprinkles of joy, let's enjoy the ride!
Stardust in pockets, we'll shine out our light,
In this funny cosmos, all worries take flight!

So here's to the magic, of silly delight,
With connections that sparkle, so brilliantly bright!
In this stellar ballet, we glide and we sway,
Together in laughter, forever we'll play!

www.ingramcontent.com/pod-product-compliance
Ingram Content Group UK Ltd.
Pitfield, Milton Keynes, MK11 3LW, UK
UKHW020634240225
4728UKWH00003B/155